AWESOME ATHLETES

ALEX RODRIGUEZ

Joe Christensen

ABDO Publishing Company

visit us at
www.abdopub.com

Published by ABDO Publishing Company, 4940 Viking Drive, Edina, Minnesota 55435.
Copyright © 2004 by Abdo Consulting Group, Inc. International copyrights reserved in all
countries. No part of this book may be reproduced in any form without written permission from
the publisher.

Printed in the United States.

Cover Photo: Corbis
Interior Photos: Corbis pp. 14, 15, 17, 23, 29; Getty Images pp. 9, 14, 19, 21, 27; *Sports
Illustrated* pp. 5, 7, 11, 13, 24, 31

Editor: Tamara L. Britton
Art Direction: Jessica A. Klein

Library of Congress Cataloging-in-Publication Data

Christensen, Joe, 1973-
   Alex Rodriguez / Joe Christensen.
      p. cm. -- (Awesome athletes)
   Includes index.
   Summary: An introduction to the life and career of Alex Rodriguez, baseball star.
   ISBN 1-59197-485-2
   1. Rodriguez, Alex, 1975---Juvenile literature. 2. Baseball players--United States--
Biography--Juvenile literature. [1. Rodriguez, Alex, 1975- 2. Baseball players. 3. Dominican
Americans--Biography.] I. Title. II. Series.

GV865.R62C57 2003
796.357'092--dc21
   [B]   2003044378

Contents

The Best and the Brightest

Throw Alex Rodriguez a baseball, and he'll catch it. Throw him a question about baseball history, and he'll answer it. Throw him a fastball down the middle, and he'll probably hit a home run.

His fans call him A-Rod. His friends used to call him Cheech. Some **critics** call him greedy. But, even the grouchy ones say he's one of the best players in the game.

Throw Alex a hanging curveball, and he'll crush it. Throw him a pop fly, and he's right under it. Throw him some bad news, like the time his mom told him his dad had moved away, and he'll still make the best of it.

Alex makes everything look easy. He plays shortstop, the hardest position in baseball, and almost never makes an error.

Until about 10 years ago, most shortstops were wimpy, little guys who could barely hit the ball over the fence. They had nicknames like Pee Wee and Scooter.

In 2002, Alex had 57 home runs—more than Barry Bonds, more than Sammy Sosa, more than any other player in baseball that year.

Alex seems to have it all. He makes more money with the Texas Rangers than any **professional** athlete in a team sport. His earnings are $25 million per season, or about $150,000 per game. He has movie-star good looks and a teacher's brain.

But talk to anyone who knows him, and they aren't jealous. He's too nice to make them feel that way. He remembers when nothing came easily. He remembers when his mom had to work two jobs to support his family. He appreciates hard work.

Ricky Ledee, who played with Alex in Texas, told *Sporting News Magazine* that Alex was "the best teammate I've ever had."

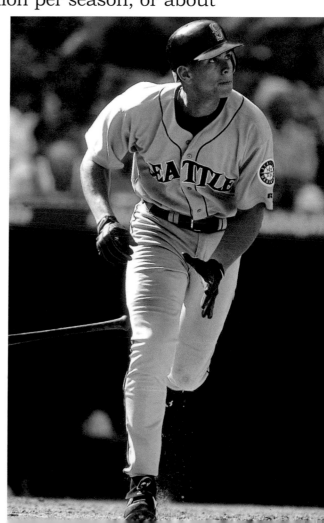

Alex rounds the bases after slugging a home run.

Early Setbacks

The score is tied with two outs in the bottom of the ninth. Alex Rodriguez is at the plate. But, this is not how Alex defines pressure.

"Pressure to me is when you have to pay the rent at the end of the month, and you don't know where the next dollar's coming from," he told CNN. "And I've been there before."

Alex was born July 27, 1975, in New York, New York. His father, Victor, owned a shoe store there. When Alex was four, the family moved to the Dominican Republic. It is an island nation that sits a few hundred miles southeast of Florida. Four years later, Victor moved the family to Miami, where he opened another shoe store. Then everything changed.

When Alex was nine, Victor left the family in Miami and moved to New York. That left Alex's mother to raise Alex, his older sister, Susy, and his older brother, Joe.

Alex wouldn't hear from his father again until the day the Seattle Mariners made Alex the number one pick in the 1993 **draft**. His father's absence made Alex angry and sad.

Alex had to work through his parents' divorce, and he had his own issues to deal with. He was funny, but he was skinny. The other kids nicknamed him Cheech.

Surrounded by trouble in Miami, Alex could have easily fallen into drugs and alcohol. Instead, he fell in love with baseball.

Alex runs for the ball.

Mom: The Biggest Inspiration

When Alex's father left his life, some very important people were there to help. But, none had a bigger impact than his mother, Lourdes.

She worked as a secretary by day and as a waitress by night to pay the bills. Eventually, she owned a business office and restaurant.

"My mom is hard-working and smart," Alex said. "I owe so much to her."

Alex learned his work **ethic** from his mother. It is a work ethic that still shows today. If the Rangers have a game that starts at 7:00 P.M., he is usually at the ballpark by 1:30 in the afternoon, taking batting practice and studying his swing on videotape.

Right before the game, he's one of the few players out on the field playing catch. It's a long season, with 162 games, and sometimes big-league players jog to first base when they hit a routine ground ball. Not Alex. He's always hustling, always giving it his best.

Alex also learned from his mother that it was okay to dream. From a young age, Alex wore the number 3 on his uniform like one of his childhood heroes, Atlanta Braves outfielder Dale Murphy. Above his bed, Alex hung a poster of another hero, Baltimore Orioles shortstop Cal Ripken Jr. Little did Alex know that someday he would become Ripken's good friend.

Alex hustles through an obstacle course during spring training.

Finding His Focus

Alex Rodriguez was lucky. He may not have had a father at home, but he had good people in his life. He liked football, basketball, and baseball. So a friend's father brought him to the Boys & Girls Clubs of Miami, the same playground where major leaguers such as Jose Canseco and Rafael Palmeiro once shined.

Alex is a superstar baseball player. But, people who used to watch him play basketball think he could have become a National Basketball Association point guard. He is six feet, three inches tall and has tremendous athletic ability.

Alex played basketball in high school, as well as football. But, his mom wanted him to play only two sports, so he would have more time to study. Alex decided to give up basketball. Soon after, he gave up football, too. He wanted to focus on baseball, his favorite sport.

Opposite page: Alex plays for his high school, Westminster Christian.

High School Champion

There's an old saying that when the student is ready, the teacher will emerge. For Alex Rodriguez, that teacher was Rich Hofman, his high school baseball coach at Miami's Westminster Christian.

When Hofman first laid eyes on Alex, he saw a scrawny, 165-pound freshman. What Alex lacked in muscle, however, he made up for with his enthusiasm.

But, he was still a fairly average player as a sophomore. After that season, Hofman gave him a pep talk. He told Alex to start running and lifting weights. He told him to eat right and build up his body. And he gave him a goal.

Stay focused, Hofman told him, and you'll become an all-American as a junior. And by the time you're a senior, Hofman said, you'll become the nation's number one **draft** pick.

Alex was stunned. He had considered quitting baseball, and he couldn't believe how much this man believed in him. Eventually, Alex believed in himself.

After practice, when the other players went home, Alex went to the weight room. He didn't drink. He didn't smoke. He didn't load up on junk food.

Sure enough, Hofman had it right. In Alex's junior season, with a team that also included Minnesota Twins first baseman Doug Mientkiewicz, Westminster went 33-2 and won the Florida state championship.

The Seattle Mariners had the first pick in the 1993 **draft**, and by then, everyone knew who they were going to pick. Alex's life was about to drastically change.

Alex turns a 6-3 double play.

Alex is one of the best players in baseball today.

1975	1992	1993	1996
Born July 27 in New York, New York	Leads Westminster Christian to the Florida state championship	Drafted number one by the Seattle Mariners	Leads American League with .358 batting average

How Awesome Is He?

Alex led the league in home runs in the 2002 season. See how his stats compare to those of other premier shortstops.

Player	Batting Average	Total Home Runs
Nomar Garciaparra	.310	24
Derek Jeter	.297	18
Alex Rodriguez	**.300**	**57**
Miguel Tejada	.308	34
Omar Vizquel	.275	14

ALEX RODRIGUEZ

TEAM: TEXAS RANGERS
NUMBER: 3
POSITION: SHORTSTOP
HEIGHT: 6 FEET, 3 INCHES
WEIGHT: 210 POUNDS

2000	2001	2002	2002
Signs 10-year, $252 million contract to play for the Texas Rangers	Plays All-Star Game with hero Cal Ripken Jr.	Wins the Gold Glove Award	Hits more home runs than any other player this year

- First player in the history of the Mariners with 30+ homers and steals in a season
- 2000 Major League Player of the Year
- 2002 American League leader in homers, runs, and total bases
- Five-time All-Star Game starter

Highlights

The Choice

Alex got two phone calls on June 3, 1993. One was from the Seattle Mariners, telling him he was the number one pick in the **draft**. The other was from his father, who hadn't spoken with Alex in nine years.

The timing bothered Alex, but he and his father began to patch together their relationship. However, if Alex was going to listen to anyone, it was his mother. And, she thought he should go to college.

Alex had a decision to make. He had accepted a **scholarship** from the University of Miami and enrolled in classes. But, the Mariners were ready to make him a very rich young man if he was willing to sign a **professional** contract.

School had always been important to Alex. When he was younger, he had thought about being a doctor or a lawyer. But, he also really wanted the chance to play in the major leagues.

A few hours before he was to begin his first college class, the Mariners offered him $1.3 million. That is a lot of money for anybody, let alone a recent high school graduate. It was enough to convince Alex, and eventually, he convinced his mom. But first, he made her a promise. Someday, he told her, he would go back to college.

With all his new money, Alex could have gone on a spending spree. Instead he made one big purchase, a $34,000 Jeep Cherokee, and forced himself not to spend more than $1,000 per month.

Before long, those dollar amounts would look like pocket change.

Alex waits for the pitch.

Seattle Sensation

To no one's surprise, it didn't take Alex long to make the jump from high school baseball to the major leagues. He flew through the system, playing just 168 minor league games before he became a regular in the Seattle lineup.

In 1996, Alex played his first full major league season, and what a season it was! He led the American League with a .358 batting average and finished second in the Most Valuable Player voting behind Juan Gonzalez.

The American League hadn't seen a right-handed hitter post a higher average since Joe DiMaggio hit .381 for the New York Yankees in 1939. Alex became the first shortstop to win a batting title in 52 years. And to think, he was still only 21 years old.

Those were special days for the Mariners's fans. They got to watch three of the greatest players in the game— Alex, Ken Griffey Jr., and Randy Johnson.

Seattle had never seen such enthusiasm for its baseball team. Fans flocked to the Kingdome, a faceless old pile of cement. Eventually, the city was inspired to build the beautiful new stadium, Safeco Field.

Alex dives for a ground ball.

The Biggest Payday

For Seattle Mariners' fans, it was too good to last. They watched Alex thrive for six seasons, until he eventually became too good for the team to afford. After a player spends six years in the major leagues, he has the right to play for any team by becoming a free agent.

When Alex became a free agent after the 2000 season, every team in baseball wished for the chance to sign him. But only a few teams could afford it. Seattle tried, and so did the New York Mets. But in the end, their bids fell well short of that of the Texas Rangers.

On December 11, 2000, Alex signed a 10-year contract with the Rangers for $252 million. It was the richest contract in sports history. To put it into perspective, consider that Rangers owner Tom Hicks spent $250 million to buy the team in 1998. Hicks spent $2 million more on Alex than he had for the entire team.

Critics said Alex's contract would ruin baseball, and they called it the ultimate example of player greed. Sometimes he still hears the crowds booing his name, especially in Seattle. All he can do is shrug his shoulders and keep doing his best.

"I'm almost embarrassed and ashamed of this contract," he told CNN. "This is a game I would pay to play."

Alex tries on his new team jersey after being introduced to the media as the Texas Rangers's new shortstop.

Honoring Cal

Money hasn't spoiled Alex Rodriguez. That became clear at the 2001 All-Star Game. If one moment could sum up Alex's personality, this was it. That night, he showed his childhood hero, Cal Ripken Jr., the ultimate form of respect.

In 1997, after 15 brilliant years at shortstop for the Baltimore Orioles, Ripken had moved to third base. This was to be Ripken's final All-Star Game, and everyone wanted to do something special for him.

Fans had voted for Alex to start at shortstop for the American League, and Ripken was supposed to start at third base. But as soon as they took the field, Alex started motioning for Ripken to switch positions with him. At first, Ripken didn't want to do it. But then he saw American League manager Joe Torre motioning from the dugout. Alex had shared his plan with Torre before the game. Torre thought it was a great idea.

Alex had grown up with Ripken's poster above his bed. He had awoken each morning as a child and done a Ripken-like workout—100 push-ups and 100 sit-ups. He had visited Ripken's home as a young player to learn how to handle superstardom. Alex soaked up his words like a sponge.

Alex wasn't going to let the game start unless Ripken returned to his rightful place at shortstop. "It was a really neat tribute," Ripken said.

Alex asks Cal Ripken Jr. to switch positions at the 2001 All-Star Game.

Building His Own Legend

Alex went to the playoffs three times with the Seattle Mariners, but he has never been to the World Series. His good friend, New York Yankees shortstop Derek Jeter, has teased him about this over the years. Jeter, a very good shortstop in his own right, has already won four World Series titles.

This has become a golden era for shortstops. Ripken seemed to change the position, adding home

Alex with good friend Derek Jeter

run power to a spot normally reserved for players with weak bats and strong gloves.

Oakland Athletics shortstop Miguel Tejada edged Alex for the 2002 American League MVP award. Other premier shortstops include Boston's Nomar Garciaparra and Cleveland's Omar Vizquel.

But in terms of performance, Alex stands alone. He hit 52 and 57 home runs his first two years in Texas. No shortstop in the history of baseball had ever hit more than 47. Alex also won the Gold Glove Award in 2002 as the top defensive player at his position.

On April 2, 2003, Alex made history again by becoming the youngest player ever to hit his 300th home run. Alex was 27 years, 249 days old. The previous player to hold this record was Jamie Foxx at 27 years, 328 days old.

The Rangers finished in last place in both the 2001 and 2002 seasons, but it hasn't changed Alex's commitment. Entering the 2003 season, he had played in 386 **consecutive** games.

Cal Ripken Jr. is called "the Ironman" because he holds baseball's record of 2,632 consecutive games played. Alex is looking more and more like his hero every year.

Off the Diamond

Life just keeps getting better for this star shortstop. On November 2, 2002, Alex married his longtime girlfriend Cynthia Scurtis. Cynthia is a high school psychology teacher in Miami.

When he's not playing baseball, Alex enjoys basketball, golf, and boating. He has season tickets for both the Dallas Mavericks and the Dallas Stars.

And, Alex is keeping his promise to his mother. He is spending his off-seasons at the University of Miami. He hopes to earn a degree in business and finance.

**Opposite page: Alex
and his wife, Cynthia**

Worth Every Penny

Fortune, fame, and success sometimes combine to bring out the worst in a **professional** athlete. These days, the sports pages are filled with stories about players getting into trouble in one form or another.

Not Alex. He's never in the news for the wrong reasons. He signs hundreds of autographs every day. He calls his mother his greatest inspiration. He still goes back to Miami to see his old high school coach, Rich Hofman.

As a child, Alex liked watching University of Miami baseball games so much, he would sometimes sneak into their ballpark by jumping over a fence. He could have played there himself, but the Seattle Mariners lured him away to the pros.

That didn't stop Alex from giving something back to his favorite college team. In 2002, he made a $3.9 million donation for the university to rebuild its baseball stadium. The school plans to name it Alex Rodriguez Park.

Opposite page: Alex signs autographs for his fans.

Alex also gives millions of dollars to children's charities, and he's been a national spokesperson for the Boys & Girls Clubs of America.

"My mom always said, 'I don't care if you turn out to be a terrible ballplayer, I just want you to be a good person,'" Alex told *Sports Illustrated*. "That's the most important thing to me."

Glossary

consecutive - following one after the other in order.

critic - someone who judges the value of something.

draft - an event during which baseball teams choose amateur players to play on their team.

ethic - belief in a set system of moral values.

professional - working for money rather than pleasure.

scholarship - a gift of money to help a student pay for instruction.

Web Sites

To learn more about Alex Rodriguez, visit ABDO Publishing Company on the World Wide Web at **www.abdopub.com**. Web sites about Alex Rodriguez are featured on our Book Links page. These links are routinely monitored and updated to provide the most current information available.

Alex Rodriguez safely steals
second base in a game
against the Mariners.

Index